AF718751

Last Will and Testament

BE IT KNOWN that I, ______________________________ [Name of Testator], a resident of ______________________________, County of______________, in the State of ______________________, being of sound and disposing mind and memory and over the age of eighteen (18) years, and not being actuated by any duress, menace, fraud, mistake or undue influence, do make, publish and declare this to be my last Will and Testament, hereby revoking all my prior Wills and Codicils at any time made.

I. MARRIAGE AND CHILDREN:

I am married to ______________________, and all references in this Will to my ____________ [husband or wife] are references to ___________ [him or her]. I have the following children:

Name:______________________________Date of Birth:____________
Name: ______________________________Date of Birth:____________
Name: ______________________________Date of Birth:____________
Name: ______________________________Date of Birth:____________

II. EXECUTOR:

I appoint______________________________of ______________________ ______________________, as Executor of this my Last Will and Testament and provide that if this Executor is unable or unwilling to serve then I appoint______________________________ of______________________________, as alternate Executor. My Executor shall be authorized to carry out all provisions of this Will and pay my just debts, obligations and funeral expenses. I further provide my Executor shall not be required to post surety bond in this or any other jurisdiction, and direct that no expert appraisal be made of my estate unless required by law.

III. GUARDIAN:

In the event I shall die as the sole parent of minor children, then I appoint______________________ ______________________as Guardian of said minor children. If this named Guardian is unable or unwilling to serve, then I appoint______________________________ as alternate Guardian.

IV. BEQUESTS:

I direct that after payment of all my just debts, my property be bequeathed in the manner following:

Name:______________________________Address:______________________
Relationship:______________________________Property:______________________
____
____

Name:______________________________Address:______________________
Relationship:______________________________Property:______________________
____
____

Name:______________________________ Address:______________________________
Relationship:______________________________ Property:______________________________
____
____

Name:______________________________ Address:______________________________
Relationship:______________________________ Property:______________________________
____
____

V. SIMULTANEOUS DEATH OF SPOUSE:

In the event that my ______________ [husband or wife] shall die simultaneously with me or there is no direct evidence to establish that my______________[husband or wife] and I died other than simultaneously, I direct that ______________ [I or my husband or wife] shall be deemed to have predeceased______________ [me or my husband or wife], notwithstanding any provision of law to the contrary, and that the provisions of my Will shall be construed on such presumption.

VI. SIMULTANEOUS DEATH OF BENEFICIARY:

If any beneficiary of this Will, including any beneficiary or any trust established by this Will, other than my______________ [husband or wife], shall die within 60 days of my death or prior to the distribution of my estate, I hereby declare that I shall be deemed to have survived such person.

VII. ALL REMAINING PROPERTY; RESIDUARY CLAUSE:

I give, devise and bequeath all of the rest, residue and remainder of my estate, of whatever kind and character, and wherever located, to my ______________ [husband or wife], provided that my ______________ [husband or wife] survives me. I make no provision for my children, knowing that, as their parent, my ______________ [husband or wife] will continue to be mindful of their needs and requirements. If my______________ [husband or wife] does not survive me, then I give, devise and bequeath all of the rest, residue and remainder of my estate, of whatever kind and character, and wherever located, to my children per share, but if any child predeceases me, then his or her share will pass, per share, to his or her lineal descendants, natural or adopted, if any, who survive me; but if there are none, then his or her share will lapse and pass equally as part of the shares of my other named children; but if none of my named children survives me or leaves a lineal descendant who survives me, then according to the order of intestate succession in the State of   .

VIII. ADDITIONAL POWERS OF THE EXECUTOR:

My Executor shall have the following additional powers with respect to my estate, to be exercised from time to time at my Executor's discretion without further license or order of any court: ______________________________
____
____
____
____
____
____
____
____

SOCRATES™
KNOW HOW MADE E-Z

4 LEGAL FORMS &
STEP-BY-STEP INSTRUCTIONS

PERSONAL

Last Will & Testament
Made E-Z

Form LF235

Make sure your last wishes are carried out, leave your heirs clear and specific instructions and give yourself peace of mind. This easy-to-use form makes it simple and affordable to execute your own will.

Contents reviewed and approved by licensed attorneys

Know how to do more yourself and save

Customer service at **www.socrates.com** or toll-free 1.800.SOCRATES

SEE FORM ON BACK

IX. OPTIONAL PROVISIONS:

I have placed my initials next to the provisions below that I adopt as part of this Will. Any unmarked provision is not adopted by me and is not part of this Will.

________ If any beneficiary to this Will is indebted to me at the time of my death, and the beneficiary evidences this debt by a valid Promissory Note payable to me, then such person's portion of my estate shall be diminished by the amount of such debt.

________ Any and all debts of my estate shall first be paid from my residuary estate. Any debts on any real property bequeathed in this Will shall be assumed by the person to receive such real property and not paid by my Executor.

________ I direct that my remains be cremated and that the ashes be disposed of according to the wishes of my Executor.

________ I direct that my remains be cremated and that the ashes be disposed of in the following manner: ________________
____
____
____

________ I desire to be buried in the____ cemetery in______________________________County, ____.

X. SEVERABILITY AND SURVIVAL

If any part of this Will is declared invalid, illegal or inoperative for any reason, it is my intent that the remaining parts shall be effective and fully operative, and that any Court so interpreting this Will and any provision in it construe in favor of survival.

Testator's Initials: ______________________________

Execute and attest before a notary.
Caution: Louisiana residents should consult an attorney before preparing a will.

IN WITNESS WHEREOF, I have hereunto set my hand this________ day of ________________________, ________________(year), to this my Last Will and Testament.

Testator Signature: ______________________________

XI. WITNESSED:

The testator has signed this will at the end and on each other separate page, and has declared or signified in our presence that it is his/her last will and testament, and in the presence of the testator and each other we have hereunto subscribed our names this ___________day of ________________________ , 20______.

Witness Signature: ____

Address: ____
____

Witness Signature: ____

Address: ____

____

Witness Signature: ____

Address: ____

____

ACKNOWLEDGMENT

State of }
County of

We, ______________________________, ______________________________,
______________________________, and ______________________________,
the testator and the witnesses, respectively, whose names are signed to the attached and foregoing instrument, were sworn and declared to the undersigned that the testator signed the instrument as his/her Last Will and that each of the witnesses, in the presence of the testator and each other, signed the will as a witness.

Testator:______________________________ Witness: ______________________________
Witness: ______________________________
Witness: ______________________________

On______________________________before me, ______________________________, appeared ______________________________personally known to me (or proved to me on the basis of satisfactory evidence) to be the person(s) whose name(s) is/are subscribed to the within instrument and acknowledged to me that he/she/they executed the same in his/her/their authorized capacity(ies), and that by his/her/their signature(s) on the instrument the person(s), or the entity upon behalf of which the person(s) acted, executed the instrument.
WITNESS my hand and official seal.

Signature of Notary: ____

Affiant _____Known_____Produced ID
Type of ID______________________
(Seal)

Last Will and Testament

BE IT KNOWN that I, ____ [Name of Testator], a resident of ______________________________________, County of______________, in the State of ____________________________, being of sound and disposing mind and memory and over the age of eighteen (18) years, and not being actuated by any duress, menace, fraud, mistake or undue influence, do make, publish and declare this to be my last Will and Testament, hereby revoking all my prior Wills and Codicils at any time made.

I. MARRIAGE AND CHILDREN:

I am married to ______________________________ , and all references in this Will to my ___________ [husband or wife] are references to __________ [him or her]. I have the following children:

Name:____Date of Birth:___________

Name: ____Date of Birth:___________

Name: ____Date of Birth:___________

Name: ____Date of Birth:___________

II. EXECUTOR:

I appoint__________________________________of ___________________ _____________________, as Executor of this my Last Will and Testament and provide that if this Executor is unable or unwilling to serve then I appoint____ of____, as alternate Executor. My Executor shall be authorized to carry out all provisions of this Will and pay my just debts, obligations and funeral expenses. I further provide my Executor shall not be required to post surety bond in this or any other jurisdiction, and direct that no expert appraisal be made of my estate unless required by law.

III. GUARDIAN:

In the event I shall die as the sole parent of minor children, then I appoint_______________________ ______________________________as Guardian of said minor children. If this named Guardian is unable or unwilling to serve, then I appoint____ as alternate Guardian.

IV. BEQUESTS:

I direct that after payment of all my just debts, my property be bequeathed in the manner following:

Name:________________________________Address:_________________________

Relationship:__________________________Property:________________________

____

____

Name:________________________________Address:_________________________

Relationship:__________________________Property:________________________

____

____

Name:____Address:____________________________
Relationship:____Property:___________________________

____

____

Name:____Address:____________________________
Relationship:____Property:___________________________

____

____

V. SIMULTANEOUS DEATH OF SPOUSE:

In the event that my _______________ [husband or wife] shall die simultaneously with me or there is no direct evidence to establish that my_______________[husband or wife] and I died other than simultaneously, I direct that _______________ [I or my husband or wife] shall be deemed to have predeceased________________ [me or my husband or wife], notwithstanding any provision of law to the contrary, and that the provisions of my Will shall be construed on such presumption.

VI. SIMULTANEOUS DEATH OF BENEFICIARY:

If any beneficiary of this Will, including any beneficiary or any trust established by this Will, other than my_____________ [husband or wife], shall die within 60 days of my death or prior to the distribution of my estate, I hereby declare that I shall be deemed to have survived such person.

VII. ALL REMAINING PROPERTY; RESIDUARY CLAUSE:

I give, devise and bequeath all of the rest, residue and remainder of my estate, of whatever kind and character, and wherever located, to my _____________ [husband or wife], provided that my _____________ [husband or wife] survives me. I make no provision for my children, knowing that, as their parent, my _____________ [husband or wife] will continue to be mindful of their needs and requirements. If my_____________ [husband or wife] does not survive me, then I give, devise and bequeath all of the rest, residue and remainder of my estate, of whatever kind and character, and wherever located, to my children per share, but if any child predeceases me, then his or her share will pass, per share, to his or her lineal descendants, natural or adopted, if any, who survive me; but if there are none, then his or her share will lapse and pass equally as part of the shares of my other named children; but if none of my named children survives me or leaves a lineal descendant who survives me, then according to the order of intestate succession in the State of .

VIII. ADDITIONAL POWERS OF THE EXECUTOR:

My Executor shall have the following additional powers with respect to my estate, to be exercised from time to time at my Executor's discretion without further license or order of any court: _______________________________________

____

____

____

____

____

____

____

____

IX. OPTIONAL PROVISIONS:

I have placed my initials next to the provisions below that I adopt as part of this Will. Any unmarked provision is not adopted by me and is not part of this Will.

________ If any beneficiary to this Will is indebted to me at the time of my death, and the beneficiary evidences this debt by a valid Promissory Note payable to me, then such person's portion of my estate shall be diminished by the amount of such debt.

________ Any and all debts of my estate shall first be paid from my residuary estate. Any debts on any real property bequeathed in this Will shall be assumed by the person to receive such real property and not paid by my Executor.

________ I direct that my remains be cremated and that the ashes be disposed of according to the wishes of my Executor.

________ I direct that my remains be cremated and that the ashes be disposed of in the following manner: ________________
____
____
____

________ I desire to be buried in the ____ cemetery in__________________________County, ____.

X. SEVERABILITY AND SURVIVAL

If any part of this Will is declared invalid, illegal or inoperative for any reason, it is my intent that the remaining parts shall be effective and fully operative, and that any Court so interpreting this Will and any provision in it construe in favor of survival.

Testator's Initials: ______________________________

Execute and attest before a notary.
Caution: Louisiana residents should consult an attorney before preparing a will.

IN WITNESS WHEREOF, I have hereunto set my hand this________ day of _________________________, ________________(year), to this my Last Will and Testament.

Testator Signature: ______________________________

XI. WITNESSED:

The testator has signed this will at the end and on each other separate page, and has declared or signified in our presence that it is his/her last will and testament, and in the presence of the testator and each other we have hereunto subscribed our names this ___________day of _________________________ , 20______.

Witness Signature: ____

Address: ____
____

Witness Signature: ____

Address: ____

____

Witness Signature: ____

Address: ____

____

ACKNOWLEDGMENT

State of }
County of }

We, ______________________________________, ______________________________________,
______________________________________, and ______________________________________,
the testator and the witnesses, respectively, whose names are signed to the attached and foregoing instrument, were sworn and declared to the undersigned that the testator signed the instrument as his/her Last Will and that each of the witnesses, in the presence of the testator and each other, signed the will as a witness.

Testator:______________________________ Witness: ______________________________

Witness: ______________________________

Witness: ______________________________

On____________________________before me, ______________________________, appeared ______________________________________personally known to me (or proved to me on the basis of satisfactory evidence) to be the person(s) whose name(s) is/are subscribed to the within instrument and acknowledged to me that he/she/they executed the same in his/her/their authorized capacity(ies), and that by his/her/their signature(s) on the instrument the person(s), or the entity upon behalf of which the person(s) acted, executed the instrument.
WITNESS my hand and official seal.

Signature of Notary: ____

Affiant _____Known_____Produced ID

Type of ID______________________

(Seal)

Last Will and Testament

BE IT KNOWN that I, ____ [Name of Testator], a resident of ____, County of______________, in the State of ____________________________, being of sound and disposing mind and memory and over the age of eighteen (18) years, and not being actuated by any duress, menace, fraud, mistake or undue influence, do make, publish and declare this to be my last Will and Testament, hereby revoking all my prior Wills and Codicils at any time made.

I. MARRIAGE AND CHILDREN:

I am married to ______________________________ , and all references in this Will to my ____________ [husband or wife] are references to __________ [him or her]. I have the following children:

Name:____Date of Birth:____________

Name: ____Date of Birth:____________

Name: ____Date of Birth:____________

Name: ____Date of Birth:____________

II. EXECUTOR:

I appoint____of ____________________ ____________________, as Executor of this my Last Will and Testament and provide that if this Executor is unable or unwilling to serve then I appoint____ of____, as alternate Executor. My Executor shall be authorized to carry out all provisions of this Will and pay my just debts, obligations and funeral expenses. I further provide my Executor shall not be required to post surety bond in this or any other jurisdiction, and direct that no expert appraisal be made of my estate unless required by law.

III. GUARDIAN:

In the event I shall die as the sole parent of minor children, then I appoint______________________ ______________________________as Guardian of said minor children. If this named Guardian is unable or unwilling to serve, then I appoint____ as alternate Guardian.

IV. BEQUESTS:

I direct that after payment of all my just debts, my property be bequeathed in the manner following:

Name:____Address:____________________________

Relationship:_________________________________Property:___________________________

____

____

Name:____Address:____________________________

Relationship:_________________________________Property:___________________________

____

____

Name:____Address:______________________________

Relationship:_______________________________________Property:_____________________________

____

____

Name:____Address:______________________________

Relationship:_______________________________________Property:_____________________________

____

____

V. SIMULTANEOUS DEATH OF SPOUSE:

In the event that my ______________ [husband or wife] shall die simultaneously with me or there is no direct evidence to establish that my______________[husband or wife] and I died other than simultaneously, I direct that ______________ [I or my husband or wife] shall be deemed to have predeceased_______________ [me or my husband or wife], notwithstanding any provision of law to the contrary, and that the provisions of my Will shall be construed on such presumption.

VI. SIMULTANEOUS DEATH OF BENEFICIARY:

If any beneficiary of this Will, including any beneficiary or any trust established by this Will, other than my_____________ [husband or wife], shall die within 60 days of my death or prior to the distribution of my estate, I hereby declare that I shall be deemed to have survived such person.

VII. ALL REMAINING PROPERTY; RESIDUARY CLAUSE:

I give, devise and bequeath all of the rest, residue and remainder of my estate, of whatever kind and character, and wherever located, to my _____________ [husband or wife], provided that my _____________ [husband or wife] survives me. I make no provision for my children, knowing that, as their parent, my _____________ [husband or wife] will continue to be mindful of their needs and requirements. If my_____________ [husband or wife] does not survive me, then I give, devise and bequeath all of the rest, residue and remainder of my estate, of whatever kind and character, and wherever located, to my children per share, but if any child predeceases me, then his or her share will pass, per share, to his or her lineal descendants, natural or adopted, if any, who survive me; but if there are none, then his or her share will lapse and pass equally as part of the shares of my other named children; but if none of my named children survives me or leaves a lineal descendant who survives me, then according to the order of intestate succession in the State of .

VIII. ADDITIONAL POWERS OF THE EXECUTOR:

My Executor shall have the following additional powers with respect to my estate, to be exercised from time to time at my Executor's discretion without further license or order of any court: ______________________________________

____

____

____

____

____

____

____

____

IX. OPTIONAL PROVISIONS:

I have placed my initials next to the provisions below that I adopt as part of this Will. Any unmarked provision is not adopted by me and is not part of this Will.

________ If any beneficiary to this Will is indebted to me at the time of my death, and the beneficiary evidences this debt by a valid Promissory Note payable to me, then such person's portion of my estate shall be diminished by the amount of such debt.

________ Any and all debts of my estate shall first be paid from my residuary estate. Any debts on any real property bequeathed in this Will shall be assumed by the person to receive such real property and not paid by my Executor.

________ I direct that my remains be cremated and that the ashes be disposed of according to the wishes of my Executor.

________ I direct that my remains be cremated and that the ashes be disposed of in the following manner: ________________
____
____
____

________ I desire to be buried in the ____ cemetery
in ______________________________ County, ______________________________________.

X. SEVERABILITY AND SURVIVAL

If any part of this Will is declared invalid, illegal or inoperative for any reason, it is my intent that the remaining parts shall be effective and fully operative, and that any Court so interpreting this Will and any provision in it construe in favor of survival.

Testator's Initials: ______________________________

Execute and attest before a notary.
Caution: Louisiana residents should consult an attorney before preparing a will.

IN WITNESS WHEREOF, I have hereunto set my hand this________ day of ______________________,
________________(year), to this my Last Will and Testament.

Testator Signature: ______________________________

XI. WITNESSED:

The testator has signed this will at the end and on each other separate page, and has declared or signified in our presence that it is his/her last will and testament, and in the presence of the testator and each other we have hereunto subscribed our names this ___________day of _________________________ , 20______.

Witness Signature: ____

Address: ____
____

Witness Signature: ____

Address: ____

____

Witness Signature: ____

Address: ____

____

ACKNOWLEDGMENT

State of }
County of }

We, ____________________________, ____________________________,

____________________________, and ____________________________,

the testator and the witnesses, respectively, whose names are signed to the attached and foregoing instrument, were sworn and declared to the undersigned that the testator signed the instrument as his/her Last Will and that each of the witnesses, in the presence of the testator and each other, signed the will as a witness.

Testator:____________________________ Witness: ____________________________

Witness: ____________________________

Witness: ____________________________

On____________________________before me, ____________________________, appeared ____________________________personally known to me (or proved to me on the basis of satisfactory evidence) to be the person(s) whose name(s) is/are subscribed to the within instrument and acknowledged to me that he/she/they executed the same in his/her/their authorized capacity(ies), and that by his/her/their signature(s) on the instrument the person(s), or the entity upon behalf of which the person(s) acted, executed the instrument.

WITNESS my hand and official seal.

Signature of Notary: ____

Affiant _____Known_____Produced ID

Type of ID________________________

(Seal)

Last Will and Testament

BE IT KNOWN that I, ____[Name of Testator], a resident of ____, County of______________, in the State of ______________________________________, being of sound and disposing mind and memory and over the age of eighteen (18) years, and not being actuated by any duress, menace, fraud, mistake or undue influence, do make, publish and declare this to be my last Will and Testament, hereby revoking all my prior Wills and Codicils at any time made.

I. MARRIAGE AND CHILDREN:

I am married to ____ , and all references in this Will to my ____________ [husband or wife] are references to ___________ [him or her]. I have the following children:

Name:____Date of Birth:____________

Name: ____Date of Birth:____________

Name: ____Date of Birth:____________

Name: ____Date of Birth:____________

II. EXECUTOR:

I appoint____of ______________________________________, as Executor of this my Last Will and Testament and provide that if this Executor is unable or unwilling to serve then I appoint____ of____, as alternate Executor. My Executor shall be authorized to carry out all provisions of this Will and pay my just debts, obligations and funeral expenses. I further provide my Executor shall not be required to post surety bond in this or any other jurisdiction, and direct that no expert appraisal be made of my estate unless required by law.

III. GUARDIAN:

In the event I shall die as the sole parent of minor children, then I appoint______________________________ ____________________________________as Guardian of said minor children. If this named Guardian is unable or unwilling to serve, then I appoint____ as alternate Guardian.

IV. BEQUESTS:

I direct that after payment of all my just debts, my property be bequeathed in the manner following:

Name:____Address:______________________________

Relationship:____Property:______________________________

____

____

Name:____Address:______________________________

Relationship:____Property:______________________________

____

____

Name:____Address:______________________________

Relationship:____Property:_____________________________

____

____

Name:____Address:______________________________

Relationship:____Property:_____________________________

____

____

V. SIMULTANEOUS DEATH OF SPOUSE:

In the event that my _____________ [husband or wife] shall die simultaneously with me or there is no direct evidence to establish that my_____________[husband or wife] and I died other than simultaneously, I direct that _____________ [I or my husband or wife] shall be deemed to have predeceased_____________ [me or my husband or wife], notwithstanding any provision of law to the contrary, and that the provisions of my Will shall be construed on such presumption.

VI. SIMULTANEOUS DEATH OF BENEFICIARY:

If any beneficiary of this Will, including any beneficiary or any trust established by this Will, other than my_____________ [husband or wife], shall die within 60 days of my death or prior to the distribution of my estate, I hereby declare that I shall be deemed to have survived such person.

VII. ALL REMAINING PROPERTY; RESIDUARY CLAUSE:

I give, devise and bequeath all of the rest, residue and remainder of my estate, of whatever kind and character, and wherever located, to my _____________ [husband or wife], provided that my _____________ [husband or wife] survives me. I make no provision for my children, knowing that, as their parent, my _____________ [husband or wife] will continue to be mindful of their needs and requirements. If my_____________ [husband or wife] does not survive me, then I give, devise and bequeath all of the rest, residue and remainder of my estate, of whatever kind and character, and wherever located, to my children per share, but if any child predeceases me, then his or her share will pass, per share, to his or her lineal descendants, natural or adopted, if any, who survive me; but if there are none, then his or her share will lapse and pass equally as part of the shares of my other named children; but if none of my named children survives me or leaves a lineal descendant who survives me, then according to the order of intestate succession in the State of .

VIII. ADDITIONAL POWERS OF THE EXECUTOR:

My Executor shall have the following additional powers with respect to my estate, to be exercised from time to time at my Executor's discretion without further license or order of any court: ______________________________

____

____

____

____

____

____

____

____

IX. OPTIONAL PROVISIONS:

I have placed my initials next to the provisions below that I adopt as part of this Will. Any unmarked provision is not adopted by me and is not part of this Will.

________ If any beneficiary to this Will is indebted to me at the time of my death, and the beneficiary evidences this debt by a valid Promissory Note payable to me, then such person's portion of my estate shall be diminished by the amount of such debt.

________ Any and all debts of my estate shall first be paid from my residuary estate. Any debts on any real property bequeathed in this Will shall be assumed by the person to receive such real property and not paid by my Executor.

________ I direct that my remains be cremated and that the ashes be disposed of according to the wishes of my Executor.

________ I direct that my remains be cremated and that the ashes be disposed of in the following manner: ________________
____
____
____

________ I desire to be buried in the____ cemetery in__________________________________County, ______________________________________.

X. SEVERABILITY AND SURVIVAL

If any part of this Will is declared invalid, illegal or inoperative for any reason, it is my intent that the remaining parts shall be effective and fully operative, and that any Court so interpreting this Will and any provision in it construe in favor of survival.

Testator's Initials: ______________________________

Execute and attest before a notary.
Caution: Louisiana residents should consult an attorney before preparing a will.

IN WITNESS WHEREOF, I have hereunto set my hand this________ day of ________________________, ________________(year), to this my Last Will and Testament.

Testator Signature: ______________________________

XI. WITNESSED:

The testator has signed this will at the end and on each other separate page, and has declared or signified in our presence that it is his/her last will and testament, and in the presence of the testator and each other we have hereunto subscribed our names this ___________day of _________________________ , 20______.

Witness Signature: ____

Address: ____
____

Witness Signature: ____

Address: ____
____

Witness Signature: ____

Address: ____
____

ACKNOWLEDGMENT

State of }
County of }

We, ________________________________, ________________________________,
________________________________, and ________________________________,
the testator and the witnesses, respectively, whose names are signed to the attached and foregoing instrument, were sworn and declared to the undersigned that the testator signed the instrument as his/her Last Will and that each of the witnesses, in the presence of the testator and each other, signed the will as a witness.

Testator:________________________________ Witness: ________________________________
Witness: ________________________________
Witness: ________________________________

On________________________before me, ________________________, appeared
________________________________personally known to me (or proved to me on the basis of satisfactory evidence) to be the person(s) whose name(s) is/are subscribed to the within instrument and acknowledged to me that he/she/they executed the same in his/her/their authorized capacity(ies), and that by his/her/their signature(s) on the instrument the person(s), or the entity upon behalf of which the person(s) acted, executed the instrument.
WITNESS my hand and official seal.

Signature of Notary: ____

Affiant _____Known_____Produced ID
Type of ID________________________
(Seal)

Name:______________________________Address:____________________
Relationship:_________________________Property:___________________

____

_____________________________ 13 _____________________________

Name:______________________________Address:____________________
Relationship:_________________________Property:___________________

____

____

V. SIMULTANEOUS DEATH OF SPOUSE:

In the event that my ____14____ [husband or wife] shall die simultaneously with me or there is no direct evidence to establish that my______________[husband or wife] and I died other than simultaneously, I direct that ______________ [I or my husband or wife] shall be deemed to have predeceased______________ [me or my husband or wife], notwithstanding any provision of law to the contrary, and that the provisions of my Will shall be construed on such presumption.

VI. SIMULTANEOUS DEATH OF BENEFICIARY:

If any beneficiary of this Will, including any beneficiary or any trust established by this Will, other than my____15____ [husband or wife], shall die within 60 days of my death or prior to the distribution of my estate, I hereby declare that I shall be deemed to have survived such person.

VII. ALL REMAINING PROPERTY; RESIDUARY CLAUSE.

I give, devise and bequeath all of the rest, residue and remainder of my estate, of whatever kind and character, and wherever located, to my ____________ [husband or wife], provided that my ____________ [husband or wife] survives me. I make no provision for my children, knowing that, as their parent, my ____________ [husband or wife] will continue to be mindful of their needs and requirements. If my____________ [husband or wife] does not survive me, then I give, devise and bequeath all of the rest, residue and remainder of my estate, of whatever kind and character, and wherever located, to my children per share, but if any child predeceases me, then his or her share will pass, per share, to his or her lineal descendants, natural or adopted, if any, who survive me; but if there are none, then his or her share will lapse and pass equally as part of the shares of my other named children; but if none of my named children survives me or leaves a lineal descendant who survives me, then according to the order of intestate succession in the State of

VIII. ADDITIONAL POWERS OF THE EXECUTOR:

My Executor shall have the following additional powers with respect to my estate, to be exercised from time to time at my Executor's discretion without further license or order of any court: ______________________________

____

____

____

_____________________________ 16 _____________________________

____

____

____

____

Page 2

www.socrates.com

IX. OPTIONAL PROVISIONS:

I have placed my initials next to the provisions below that I adopt as part of this Will. Any unmarked provision is not adopted by me and is not part of this Will.

________ If any beneficiary to this Will is indebted to me at the time of my death, and the beneficiary evidences this debt by a valid Promissory Note payable to me, then such person's portion of my estate shall be diminished by the amount of such debt.

________ Any and all debts of my estate shall first be paid from my residuary estate. Any debts on any real property bequeathed in this Will shall be assumed by the person to receive such real property and not paid by my Executor.

________ I direct that my remains be cremated and that the ashes be disposed of according to the wishes of my Executor.

________ I direct that my remains be cremated and that the ashes be disposed of in the following manner: ______________

____

____

_____________________________ 17 _____________________________

________ I desire to be buried in the__________________________________ cemetery in_______________________County, ______________________________.

X. SEVERABILITY AND SURVIVAL

If any part of this Will is declared invalid, illegal or inoperative for any reason, it is my intent that the remaining parts shall be effective and fully operative, and that any Court so interpreting this Will and any provision in it construe in favor of survival.

Testator's Initials: ____________ 18 ____________

Execute and attest before a notary.
Caution: Louisiana residents should consult an attorney before preparing a will.

IN WITNESS WHEREOF, I have hereunto set my hand this___19___ day of ____________________,
______________(year), to this my Last Will and Testament.

Testator Signature: ____20____________________

XI. WITNESSED:

The testator has signed this will at the end and on each other separate page, and has declared or signified in our presence that it is his/her last will and testament, and in the presence of the testator and each other we have hereunto subscribed our names this ___21___day of ______________________ , 20______.

Witness Signature: __22______________________________

Address: ______________________________________
____

Page 3

www.socrates.com

Witness Signature: ______________________________________

Address: ______________________________________
____

Witness Signature: ______________________________________

Address: ______________________________________
____

Witness Signature: ______________________________________

Address: ______________________________________
____

ACKNOWLEDGMENT

State of 23 24 }
County of

We, ______________________________, ______________________________,
______________________________, and ______________________________,

the testator and the witnesses, respectively, whose names are signed to the attached and foregoing instrument, were sworn and declared to the undersigned that the testator signed the instrument as his/her Last Will and that each of the witnesses, in the presence of the testator and each other, signed the will as a witness.

Testator: 25______________________ Witness: 26______________________
Witness: ______________________
Witness: ______________________

On 27______________________before me, 28______________________, appeared
29______________________personally known to me (or proved to me on the basis of satisfactory evidence) to be the person(s) whose name(s) is/are subscribed to the within instrument and acknowledged to me that he/she/they executed the same in his/her/their authorized capacity(ies), and that by his/her/their signature(s) on the instrument the person(s), or the entity upon behalf of which the person(s) acted, executed the instrument.
WITNESS my hand and official seal.

Signature of Notary: ________30______________________

Affiant _____Known_____Produced ID
Type of ID______________________
(Seal)

Page ____ of ____ pages

31

Socrates Media, LLC

4

14 Enter information regarding possible simultaneous death of spouse, if applicable.

15 Enter information regarding simultaneous death of beneficiary.

16 Enter additional powers of executor.

17 Enter optional provisions.

18 Enter testator's initials.

19 Enter date.

20 Enter testator signature.

21 Enter date witnessed.

22 Enter witnesses' signatures and addresses.

23 Enter state.

24 Enter county.

25 Enter testator's signature.

26 Enter witnesses' signatures.

27 Enter date.

28 Enter notary name.

29 Enter name of person leaving will.

30 Enter signature of notary.

31 Enter notary seal.

Last Will & Testament

Easy To Use & Complete. Simply follow the step-by-step instructions and enter the correct information in each area shown.

Last Will and Testament

BE IT KNOWN that I, ①______________________[Name of Testator], a resident of ②______________________, County of ③________, in the State of ④______________________, being of sound and disposing mind and memory and over the age of eighteen (18) years, and not being actuated by any duress, menace, fraud, mistake or undue influence, do make, publish and declare this to be my last Will and Testament, hereby revoking all my prior Wills and Codicils at any time made.

I. MARRIAGE AND CHILDREN:

I am married to ⑤______________________, and all references in this Will to my __________ [husband or wife] are references to __________ [him or her]. I have the following children:

Name:______________________Date of Birth:__________
Name:______________________Date of Birth:__________
Name:__________⑥__________Date of Birth:__________
Name:______________________Date of Birth:__________

II. EXECUTOR:

I appoint ⑦______________________ of ⑧______________________, as Executor of this my Last Will and Testament and provide that if this Executor is unable or unwilling to serve then I appoint ⑨______________________ ⑩ of ______________________, as alternate Executor. My Executor shall be authorized to carry out all provisions of this Will and pay my just debts, obligations and funeral expenses. I further provide my Executor shall not be required to post surety bond in this or any other jurisdiction, and direct that no expert appraisal be made of my estate unless required by law.

III. GUARDIAN:

In the event I shall die as the sole parent of minor children, then I appoint ⑪______________________ as Guardian of said minor children. If this named Guardian is unable or unwilling to serve, then I appoint ⑫______________________ as alternate Guardian.

IV. BEQUESTS:

I direct that after payment of all my just debts, my property be bequeathed in the manner following:

Name:______________________Address:______________________
Relationship:______________________Property:______________________
__________⑬__________

Name:______________________Address:______________________
Relationship:______________________Property:______________________

Page 1

www.socrates.com

© 2004, Socrates Media, LLC
LF235 • Rev. 04/04

Continued inside...

1. Enter name.
2. Enter address.
3. Enter county.
4. Enter state.
5. Enter name of spouse.
6. Enter name of child or children and dates of birth.
7. Enter name of executor.
8. Enter executor's address.
9. Enter alternate executor.
10. Enter alternate executor's address.
11. Enter name of guardian for minor children.
12. Enter name of alternate guardian for minor children.
13. Enter names, addresses, relationships and property to be willed for all parties designated to inherit your property (after just debts are paid).

0404-0304 | P-LF235-4

30% POST-CONSUMER FIBER

MADE IN USA

ISBN 1-59546-039-X
90000
9 781595 460394

REORDER NO. LF235
0 53926 60121 9

Socrates Media, LLC
227 West Monroe, Suite 500
Chicago, IL 60606-5055
www.socrates.com 1.800.SOCRATES (800.762.7283)